IMAGES
of America

NORTH CADDO
PARISH

IMAGES
of America

NORTH CADDO
PARISH

Sam Collier

ARCADIA
PUBLISHING

Published by Arcadia Publishing
Charleston, South Carolina

Library of Congress Catalog Card Number: 2007925398

For all general information contact Arcadia Publishing at:
Telephone 843-853-2070
Fax 843-853-0044
E-mail sales@arcadiapublishing.com
For customer service and orders:
Toll-Free 1-888-313-2665

Visit us on the Internet at www.arcadiapublishing.com

This work is dedicated to the people of north Caddo Parish, past and present. It is a relatively small geographical area constituting the very northwestern part of Louisiana and is the area of interest for the local historical society, whose members assisted in producing this book. This area has never been addressed in an historical reference book other than three written for local consumption. This work highlights the significant role the people of this area played in the region's history.

CONTENTS

ACKNOWLEDGMENTS

The contributions of many made this book possible, and it is to them that a debt of gratitude is owed. It could not have been completed in a timely manner without the assistance of the Historical Society of North Caddo and the able voluntary leadership of Betty Matthews in collecting photographs and coordinating the efforts of others, including Johnny Pistole and Mary Virginia Skaggs. The Louisiana Oil and Gas Museum, the Mooringsport Mini Museum, and the Vivian Railroad Station Museum provided historical photographs. James Allison, Melvin Giles, Hardy Hale, Lewis Borman, and the estate of Jack D. Norman made valuable historic photographic contributions. The Hosston Branch of the Shreve Memorial Library made their collection of rare photographs of the Hoss family available. The Vivian Branch of the Shreve Memorial Library made available the extensive collection of historic photographs in the estate of Lillian Horton. David Welch, the owner of a local printing company, provided assistance scanning photographs.

INTRODUCTION

North Caddo Parish, Louisiana, the Historical Society of North Caddo's area of interest, covers 325 square miles starting just above an imaginary east-west line that bisects the county south of Mooringsport. Included within the area is Caddo Lake, with its feeder and drainage bayous; Black Bayou and its distributaries; the arable, alluvial flood plain of the Red River; and the irregularly shaped remaining upland area that was dubbed "Terrapin Neck" by the earliest settlers.

The Red River logjam, which existed for a few hundred years, backed up the flow from bayous entering the river—forming lakes and bayous and creating navigable waterways. The Red River flood plain in northern Caddo Parish is bounded on the east by the river and is shaped like an arc that sweeps south beginning at the Arkansas state line and ending at the river just north of Shreveport. The flood plain is 7 or 8 miles at it's widest and was referred to as "Caddo Prairie" by 1850. Almost all of the southern third of the prairie was covered by Soda Lake, and most of the remainder to the north experienced annual flooding before the final removal of the logjam in 1873. The uplands contained massive stands of virgin timbers, and fruit, berries, fish, and game were ubiquitous and plentiful. This was part of the land of the Caddo Indians and had been so for a few thousand years. But the United States was growing and expanding westward; encroachment on these Native American lands was inevitable and unstoppable.

In 1825, Caddo Prairie Indian agent George Grey and Caddo tribal leader Chief Dehahuit defined Caddo Indian lands to be constituted of the present areas of Miller County, Arkansas, and Caddo Parish, Louisiana. The Caddo Prairie Indian Agency was located here from 1825 until 1831, and the last Native American village in Caddo was located about 10 miles west of here.

In 1835, the United States purchased about 1 million acres from the Caddo Indians for $80,000 dollars, paying $30,000 dollars in goods at the agreement signing and $10,000 cash each of the next five years. Shreveport was established in 1837 in the southern part of the parish, and in 1838, the Louisiana portion of the Caddo cession, formerly a part of Natchitoches Parish, became Caddo Parish. Because the Indian agent had been so diligent in his duties, the migration of settlers to the southwestern United States beginning after the Louisiana Purchase in 1803 was precluded in the area. Further motivating settlers to bypass the area was the Mexican Impresario system of generous land grants in the future state of Texas beginning in 1821. The result was that settlement of Caddo Parish didn't begin until 1837, some 30 years after it had begun in other parts of Louisiana and the adjoining states of Texas and Arkansas. The last payment to the Caddo for the lands was made in 1840 on a ferryboat on Caddo Lake.

For most of the next 100 years, steamboat traffic, homesteaders, plantations, subsistence farmers, logging operations, railroad and oil boomtown building, and entrepreneurs melded to define the area's unique cultural history. Today three towns and five villages are located here, while the memories of 10 historic communities remain strong.

The first settlers depended entirely upon Native American trails and the waterways to move into the area. Travel overland through the dense forests was mostly by foot and on horse. Trails from Arkansas through the area and across the southern part of the parish into Texas moved some here. By the time of the Civil War, a road led from Shreveport through the area to Lewisville, Arkansas. Other roads from the river crossed into Texas and lead south from Mooringsport; the present Louisiana Highways 167 and 538 were beginning to evolve from Native American trails into what they are today.

The first land office patents for land were sold in 1841, and the area was referred to as Caddo Prairie in the 1850 federal census, which listed some 250 residents. By the beginning of the Civil War, there were little more than 500 people living here. Steamboats plied the Mississippi and Red Rivers, paddled through bayous, and crossed Caddo Lake from the mid-1840s until about 1900, moving people and supplies into this area, east Texas, and points west. These boats also took agricultural products out of the area. Timothy Mooring began operating a ferry across Caddo Lake in 1842, developing a steamboat port on the south side of the lake, which became the town of Mooringsport. In 1830, army captain Washington Seawell dug a short canal joining two bayous in the area with passable water routes to the north and south, creating a bypass of the Red River logjam. The bypass enabled the movement of troops and supplies to Fort Towson in the Oklahoma Territory and the movement of settlers and supplies throughout the area. Some ports became small villages, but within 50 years, they all had faded into history.

The need for lumber locally and in markets to the north and west of the area resulted in four logging railroads being located in the area from the late 1800s until the 1920s. The Gate City Lumber Railroad Company ran its line from Texarkana, across part of Arkansas, and some 10 miles into the east of the parish. Another railroad out of Atlanta, Texas, in the same general area, had its southern terminus near a local village named Frog Level. A third, McCoy Logging, ran its rail into Texas and created a sawmill village at its terminus. The fourth, the Black Bayou Lumber Company, ran its railroad some 18 miles west into Texas and established Myrtis, the largest of the sawmill villages in north Caddo Parish. Work was provided, products were developed, communities were formed and died, and settlers remained. All of those logging railroads and the villages they created are now gone.

Upland southerners from most of the Southeastern states were the pioneers of the area. Most came from the North and South Carolina, Tennessee, Alabama, and Georgia. They were for the most part of Scotch-Irish heredity. The initial surge of people acquiring land patents bought large quantities, and a cross-reference to census records shows that many did not live in the area. They were wealthy land speculators for the most part, but there were some who in fact did settle in the area, establishing large plantations and farms, and soon that became the norm. The primary method of land acquisition continued to be purchase until after 1875, when the less-affluent homesteaders began to acquire land patents.

The major period of homesteading was from about 1895 until 1925, with the first decade of the 20th century representing the peak. That homesteading activity was motivated by three significant events and subsequent related activities. First, in about 1892, the Caddo Parish Levee Board was established, and its charter included the mission of land drainage. In 1895, the board began to construct levees along the bayous in Caddo Prairie. The board then entered into an extensive drainage program. The two activities closed the bayou outlets from the river, making many thousands of acres of land available to farmers, planters, and other settlers for continuous occupation and use. The levee board's activities took about 30 years, until about 1925. From the time of the purchase of the Caddo lands in 1835, it had taken 90 years to make all of the land available for use. It is no wonder that north Caddo Parish remains rural to this day.

The second significant event that brought homesteaders into the area was the coming of the railroads, beginning in the 1890s, and the related subsequent town-building activities. Two railroads were laid in the area, one along the eastern side and another along the western side. Those passenger and freight railroads became the single-most significant economic drivers in local history, establishing numerous villages and towns with six remaining today.

The Gate City Lumber Railroad Company amended its charter in 1888 and continued its logging operations into Louisiana for about the next decade. By 1895, available timber had been removed, and the Texarkana, Shreveport, and Natchez (TS&N) was chartered with the mission of building a railroad from the state line through or near Shreveport and on to the Mississippi River to a point just west of Natchez. The TS&N acquired Gate City's assets and was authorized to build telephone and telegraph lines. In late 1899, the first TS&N train ran from Texarkana to Shreveport carrying cotton. Not far behind was a passenger train carrying railroad officials and about 200 prominent residents and community leaders. Along its route, stations and depots had been constructed and named after the landowners who provided railroad rights-of-way. Around those facilities, some 11 communities sprang into being, with four remaining today as villages. After a long period of disuse, the TS&N's tracks were removed in the 1960s and 1970s.

While the TS&N had indirectly developed four permanent villages in the eastern half of the area, the Kansas City Southern Railroad (KCS) had a direct hand in developing one community in the western half. Arthur Stillwell, the visionary founder of the KCS, planned a railroad from Kansas City to the Gulf of Mexico that included the building of towns through subsidiary companies along the route. As the railroad was laid south into Louisiana, town sites were bought, cleared, laid out into streets and lots, and marketed for business and homesites. Those companies created the town of Vivian. In late 1896, the town site plat of Vivian was filed in the parish courthouse. In February 1897, the first train made the inaugural run from Texarkana through Vivian to Shreveport. In March 1897, marketing efforts were initiated to sell lots in Vivian. Seven communities grew up around KCS stations and depots and, other than the town of Vivian, only the village of Rodessa remains today.

The first oil well creating the area's petroleum industry was drilled in 1906. This third significant economic development event, the last cultural defining force, provided an incredible amount of impetus to the growing area, bringing with it more manufacturing, road building, and people as well as phenomenal growth. That success led to the establishment of the last of the towns, Oil City. A hundred years ago, local petroleum resources made millionaires of many Shreveporters and others outside of the state. The first over-the-water oil well ever drilled anywhere in the world was completed on Caddo Lake in 1911. A number of oil-field villages evolved during the 1905 to 1935 oil boom, which created the Caddo Pine Island Oil Field, but by 1950, the villages had faded into history, except for the town of Oil City. By that time, the local economy and population base was established. The industries relating to agriculture, timber, steamboat and railroad transportation networks, and petroleum had motivated people to move here and defined the economy, the hopes, and aspirations of those people. Timber and petroleum still play large roles.

The majority of the people here are descended from the settlers who arrived during the 80-year period beginning in 1840. They are a close-knit group—each community independent but bonded together by a common history. The lifestyle of the pioneers engendered for a long time —and even to some extent today—a proud, rural, and pioneering spirit. They are individuals, they sometimes live off the land, they live off the beaten path, and they harvest game and fish to feed their families. Sometimes life is rough; they work for wages and live in close family groups. They are hospitable, extremely patriotic, and have a strong Christian sense of values passed on to subsequent generations.

One

HISTORIC VILLAGES

Each of the major events and related activities that spurred growth in this area also created small, ephemeral communities whose short lives corresponded to the staying power of the economic force. About five miles southwest of Vivian, Monterey, founded in about 1845 on the Texas-Louisiana state line, was the first significant community in the area. A post office was first located there from 1851 to 1867. Monterey, a steamboat village, faded into history by 1900, when the lake and bayou levels had lowered to a depth too low to sustain traffic.

From about 1855 to 1885, the communities of Frog Level, Hale, Black Bayou, Garfield, and Missionary arose along roads or rivers, near sawmills and general stores, or near Protestant churches. All but one of those communities received postal services on Blue Star routes out of Atlanta, Texas. The coming of the railroads signaled the end of these communities.

Ten historic communities came into being around the stations and depots built by the two railroads that traversed this area. Most of those had post offices and some form of a general store. Mira, Lane, Cavett, Uni, Hayti, Dixie, and Picket, along the eastern line, flourished briefly. Along the western railroad, Myrtis and Lewis, formed in the 1880s and 1890s as sawmill towns, took on more importance when depots and post offices were located there. Ananias/Surry was established around a railroad flag station and later had a post office. The consolidation of postal services and schools in the larger villages along both rail lines ultimately spelled the end of these historic communities.

The first oil boom, beginning in 1906, populated Lewis with oil field workers and all forms of society's evils: bars, thieves, prostitutes, murderers, and horrid living conditions. Two oil company drilling speculators overcame the evil by building the village of Trees seven miles to the west for oil field workers and their families. Trees was clean and had all of the services of a vibrant village of the era. As the boom faded in the 1940s, families moved on, and as schools and postal services were consolidated, Trees became a ghost town.

The Black Bayou Lumber Company was formed in the late 1880s during the historic logging era. A subsidiary was the Black Bayou Railroad Company, which was chartered in the states of Louisiana and Texas. The railroad ultimately reached some 18 miles into Texas. One, and perhaps the only, engineer was Albert Alsup. Alsup is depicted in this 1911 photograph at the front of the engine cab in Myrtis; the other man is unidentified. (Courtesy of the Jack D. Norman estate.)

In the background of this 1910 view is the planning mill of the Black Bayou Lumber Company at Myrtis. Note the conveyor extending down to the water where the logs were mechanically grabbed and pulled into the sawmill. The unidentified man with his pet on the skiff is maneuvering a log across the millpond to be sawed. (Courtesy of the Louisiana Oil and Gas Museum.)

Leon Walton, a descendent of one of the early pioneering families of the area, is standing on the tracks of the Kansas City Southern Railroad in this 1925 photograph taken at Myrtis. To the left background is the highway bridge over the drainage of the millpond. In the right background is the Myrtis railroad depot. (Courtesy Lillian Horton estate, Vivian Branch Shreve Memorial Library; photograph provided by Mrs. Mark Walton.)

Myrtis was the name of the company town that grew up around the Black Bayou Lumber Company's sawmill location. When the timbers had been logged out by the early 1920s, workers began to move away, and the village began to diminish. It languished until the Rodessa oil boom of 1935, when the United Gas Company built a compressor station and company town there. A small part of the station is depicted in this c. 1937 photograph. (Courtesy of the Jack D. Norman estate.)

In the 1920s, telephone communications systems were being installed throughout the area. This crew is installing telephones at Myrtis. The two men on the left are unidentified; on the right is Mack Walton. To their rear is a view of the sawdust pile at the lumber mill. (Courtesy Lillian Horton estate, Vivian Branch Shreve Memorial Library; photograph provided by Mrs. Mark Walton.)

This c. 1920 photograph was taken at the Black Bayou Lumber Company sawmill at Myrtis. In the foreground are Steve Walton and Margie Turnage. Note the large sawdust pile in the background adjacent to the log railcar. (Courtesy Lillian Horton estate, Vivian Branch Shreve Memorial Library; photograph provided by Mrs. Mark Walton.)

Located at Myrtis by 1910 were a commissary, Woodmen of the World hall, cemetery, baseball park, outdoor theater consisting of logs for sitting and a screen hung from a post, medical doctor, and a church that also served as the school. Edna Evans (on the left) and Myrtis schoolteacher Vida Holloway are depicted. (Courtesy Lillian Horton estate, Vivian Branch Shreve Memorial Library; photograph provided by Mrs. Mark Walton.)

Myrtis schoolteacher Pet Davis is standing at the right center with her 1910 class. Pictured from left to right are the following: (first row) both unidentified; (second row) Dorothy Rogers, Ruth Yarborough, Lillie Murray, Avis Larry, and Annis Grunden; (third row) Guy Alsup, Drew Evans, Bennie French, Will French, Willie Murray, George Yarborough, and ? Larry; (fourth row) Liza Walton, Artie Chisholm, Paralee Orchid, Winnie Alsup, Sudie Bell Harper, and teacher Vida Holloway. (Courtesy Lillian Horton estate, Vivian Branch Shreve Memorial Library; photograph provided by Mrs. Mark Walton.)

Lewis was located four miles south of Vivian. About the time the railroad passed through in 1895, a sawmill was constructed there and, under one banner or another, remained in operation for more than 40 years. A post office was located there from 1901 to 1927. This rare photograph, taken in about 1905, depicts some of the houses and unidentified residents of the village. (Courtesy of the Jack D. Norman estate.)

The Caddo Pine Island Oil Field boom was well under way when this photograph was taken about 1915. Lewis was a transfer point from oil storage tanks to railroad tank cars for transport to refineries. Oil is being pumped into tank cars while the two unidentified workers await its completion. Just visible to the rear are some the houses of the village. (Courtesy of the Jack D. Norman estate.)

The Weaver Brothers and Thompson Company operated sawmills in a number of southern states. Their local operation was at Lewis, and it was a very large concern. This photograph, taken in 1941, shows the milling building and associated structure. Just inside, men operating the hardware can be seen. In the left background are stacks of finished lumber. (Courtesy Lillian Horton estate, Vivian Branch Shreve Memorial Library; photograph provided by M. H. Kibler.)

This 1941 picture depicts sawyers performing their jobs at the Weaver Brothers and Thompson sawmill at Lewis. Operating the hardware that rough cut the logs was dangerous, and many men lost limbs and their lives in the process. The operators are unidentified. (Courtesy Lillian Horton estate, Vivian Branch Shreve Memorial Library; photograph provided by M. H. Kibler.)

The Shoreline site of the Crystal Oil Refining Corporation was located just south of Lewis. The refinery ceased operations in 1965 and was dismantled and removed. The company's 1937 semi-professional baseball team players were, from left to right, as follows: (first row) Bob Stanton, B. Cobb, L. Densmore, Dave Bush, unidentified, Buddy Idom, and Chubby Blount; (second row) Less Phillips, Roy Idom, Ted Bounds, Herman Stacks, Troy Idom, Andy Anderson, and Max Beard. (Courtesy Lillian Horton estate, Vivian Branch Shreve Memorial Library; photograph provided by Buddy Idom.)

Shoreline's depot was built during the 1920s. From 1937 until 1940, a post office was located at Shoreline. The depot was torn down in the 1960s. To the right of the depot are some crude oil storage tanks. Note that the oil field derricks are made of steel rather than wood like the earlier ones. (Courtesy Lillian Horton estate, Vivian Branch Shreve Memorial Library; photograph provided by Jack Norman.)

Graham's camp, depicted in this early-1900s photograph, was probably located at the old steamboat village site of Monterey, and it is representative of early living conditions at historic sawmill and oil boom communities. Monterey, about five miles southwest of Vivian, was located in Texas but its eastward layout extended into Louisiana. The location was reincarnated as a place to live during the oil boom in the area after 1906. (Courtesy of the Jack D. Norman estate.)

In this 1915 photograph taken in Monterey, William Robert Player is driving his two-horse-drawn family wagon. Sitting beside Player is Walter Mathews. Behind Mathews is his sister Beatrice. Just barely discernible standing behind Player and holding on to a branch of a tree is Ora Player Matthews, probably William's sister. Standing at the right rear is Carrie Player, perhaps William's wife. (Courtesy of the Louisiana Oil and Gas Museum.)

The only photograph found of Monterey was taken in 1908, early on in the oil boom period. Written on the photograph is the following caption: "O. L. Gregg's General Merchandise Emporium and efficient corps of clerks on Land Ave and Park Place—Monterey La." It is assumed that the man standing on the left is O. L. Gregg; the clerks are unidentified. (Courtesy of the Louisiana Oil and Gas Museum.)

This is a very rare photograph taken in about 1910 of a steamboat coursing Caddo Lake. It is representative of the type of transportation prevalent on the lake and its feeder and drainage bayous from about 1845 to about the time the photograph was taken. A smaller class of steamboat was used to travel into the bayous feeding Caddo Lake. (Courtesy of the Louisiana Oil and Gas Museum.)

This 1925 scene of Trees was snapped from the top of an oil well derrick. Most of the structures located along the road at the left were houses. The village business district is located in the center and right background. In 1911, William Stiles began building an oil field village for workers on his leased land, and Joe Trees, the lessee, named village Trees in honor of his wife. (Courtesy of the Jack D. Norman estate.)

The Potter's Station School was located about three miles west of Trees in Texas. By 1914, Trees had a three-room school where some 70 children were taught. The Potter's Station School is representative of those in the area during that time. The identifications of all of the children in this 1913 photograph have been lost. The teacher's name was Annie Stuart. (Courtesy of the Jack D. Norman estate.)

Joe Trees and Mike Benedum located their Trees Oil Company headquarters in Shreveport, Louisiana. They frequently took the morning train from Shreveport and disembarked at the depot in Lewis. The Trees Oil Company field office is depicted in the right center of this 1920 photograph. After completing their field duties, the men then returned by livery to Lewis, where they caught the evening train back to Shreveport. (Courtesy of the Jack D. Norman estate.)

In 1917, some residents of Trees lived among the village's oil-production facilities. In the left center are five or six wood-framed houses for the workers, and behind those are their well-cultivated vegetable gardens. The large industrial building and adjacent tank in the right center structure are connected by pipeline to the oil well in the left foreground. Note that all of the derricks are made of wood. (Courtesy of the Jack D. Norman estate.)

The fire at Stiles No. 94 in 1913 at Trees was a remarkable disaster. The high-pressure gas in the well burned together with some oil and shot flames higher than the adjacent trees. The structures on the ground around the burning well were heat shields that allowed firefighters to approach the fire and attempt to extinguish the blaze. (Courtesy of the Louisiana Oil and Gas Museum.)

By early 1912, Trees had a general store and a post office, and eventually William Stiles built a hotel, church, doctor's office, dance pavilion, and a pool hall. The pool hall was a very popular place for the oil field workers to spend their free time, as this 1915 picture shows. No saloons or gambling houses were ever permitted in Trees, and camp followers never came there. (Courtesy of the Louisiana Oil and Gas Museum.)

Playing pool at Trees was enjoyed by many workers in 1916. William Stiles built an airdrome for movies and stage acts to diversify village amusements. Trees was unique because one person, Stiles, owned the land and every structure on it and because it was the first oil field town ever built. It had the reputation of being the cleanest and most orderly of such towns in the country. (Courtesy of the Louisiana Oil and Gas Museum.)

Two

CADDO PINE ISLAND OIL FIELD

The 1906 discovery oil well for the Caddo Pine Island Oil Field initiated a major boost in the growth of the area's population and economy, which began to rise sharply in 1895 because of increased land availability and railroad town building. New towns and villages appeared almost overnight. Oil City was born and, together with the villages of Vivian and Mooringsport, became rough and rowdy boomtowns.

Agents, promoters, speculators, and workers swarmed into the area. Shacks promoting whiskey, gambling, and women sprang up over night. Law enforcement was almost nonexistent. People rushed to find oil. They endured roads and streets jammed with traffic, horses stuck up to their bellies in the mud, crowded trains, hucksters, and an almost unbearable lifestyle.

Shotgun houses were being erected everywhere, and board planks formed sidewalks and street crossings. Drillers, roughnecks, and roustabouts lived extremely hard lives working in the oil field 10 to 12 hours a day, seven days a week, for less than $3 a day. Families suffered equal hardships living in tent cities and other crude housing that offered little more than head cover. The streets were dirt, there were no utilities, and clothes were washed outside. During heavy rains, the streets and roads became quagmires. But the potential reward was great, and everyone was undaunted.

By 1910, most of the land surrounding Caddo Lake had been leased. The oil-production community pushed for the lake to be drained, but other forces prevailed, and in 1910, the U.S. Corps of Engineers authorized the damming of the lake. The levee board then offered to lease the land under the lake's waters. In May 1911, the Gulf Refining Company completed the world's first over-the-water oil well, located on Caddo Lake. By 1917, the oil field included the southern portion of the area, and production was declining. In 1935, the Rodessa oil field's discovery oil well was completed, and that community's population jumped from about 200 to almost 8,000 by 1940. The Caddo field then covered all of north Caddo Parish.

Photographed at the 1906 discovery oil well in the Caddo field are, from left to right, the following: (seated) Will Stone, Pink Browning, and unidentified; (standing) Oscar E. Dell, Mamie Powell, Dixie Browning, Moseley Browning, M. Carl Jones, Mittie Williams, Robert Williams, three unidentified, and John Browning; (walking at left rear) J. L. Jeter. Mrs. Walter George sits on the porch of her home. (Courtesy of the Louisiana Oil and Gas Museum.)

In May 1911, Producer's Oil Company's Harrell No. 7 was completed. The crew was making final connections when gas-pressure-blown sand, traveling up the pipe, heated and ignited the gas. Four men were badly burned, and one died of his wounds. Flames roared 75 feet into the air for 30 days. An unsuccessful fire-extinguishing attempt was made by shooting 12-pound cannonballs at the base of the blaze. (Courtesy of the Louisiana Oil and Gas Museum.)

In the early days of the oil boom, the means of transporting materials was crude compared to today's standards. In 1915, in the Caddo field oxen, horses, and mules were used to pull oil-company wagons. Two eight-mule teams are moving oil boilers in this 1915 view. From left to right are W. Alsup, Hardy Lummus, and Flim Fuller. (Courtesy of the Jack D. Norman estate.)

William Robert Player is using his wagon and team to check his lease in the Pine Island field in 1914. Note the mud adhered to the wagon wheels. (Courtesy of the Louisiana Oil and Gas Museum.)

The town of Vivian is located in the center of the Caddo oil field and became a major location for oil companies, repair and engineering shops, and material storage yards. Pipe and other oil field specific supplies are being loaded from Kansas City Southern Railroad cars on to mule-drawn wagons for delivery into the oil field in 1909 at the Vivian railroad station. (Courtesy of the Jack D. Norman estate.)

Many wells blew gas, and many millions of cubic feet of it were vented to the atmosphere each month. Some caught fire, and one burned for five years near Oil City, leaving a crater 90 feet deep and 300 feet wide when it was extinguished. A gas geyser in 1912 tossed mud and water some 20 feet into the air. (Courtesy of the Jack D. Norman estate.)

30

The drilling technology in 1907 was basic and unsafe. This unidentified crew on the wooden drilling platform of a well near Oil City operated a rotary rig of the era. Note the large chain, gear, and shaft that rotate the drill stand. The exposed hardware caused numerous injuries. Both of the derricks are made of wood. (Courtesy of the Jack D. Norman estate.)

Another view of the 1927 laborious transport technique of moving oil field equipment is shown. An eight-mule team is moving a boiler in the Pine Island field. (Courtesy of the Jack D. Norman estate.)

This type of oil loading rack was prevalent throughout the Caddo field, adjacent to the two railroads that ran through the area. This 1928 view of one is at the Superior refinery, south of the town of Vivian. Note that rail lines ran on both sides of the rack so that loading oil into the rail tankers could be expedited for large shipments. (Courtesy of the Jack D. Norman estate.)

Local sawmills provided large, rough timbers for use in building drilling platforms, derricks, storage facilities, and cat walks, and to "pave" the muddy roads that were everywhere in the oil field. This unidentified 1910 crew is moving timbers to a well site in the Ferry (Caddo) Lake field. (Courtesy of the Louisiana Oil and Gas Museum.)

Another prime mover for oil field wagons and their associated loads was an eight-oxen team, as shown in 1912 in the Caddo field. This wagon is empty, but the unidentified crew is probably on its way to load out. (Courtesy of the Louisiana Oil and Gas Museum.)

This 1915 view in the Pine Island field appears to be in a war zone. Logging and oil field operations were devastating to the timbers that stood in the area. The practices that resulted in such wholesale destruction of the environment have since been outlawed. These unidentified men have probably been servicing the bilge pump used to keep the dirt pit available for use. (Courtesy of the Louisiana Oil and Gas Museum.)

In 1917, Hardy Lummus (left), Otis Waldrop (center), and Andy Miller (holding the shotgun), from the village of Hosston, were crewmen, moving boilers and other heavy equipment in the oil field. During the day, workers like these typically hunted deer, rabbit, squirrel, and other game to be taken home and eaten for their evening meal. (Courtesy of the Jack D. Norman estate.)

This photograph was taken in 1913 of the Louisiana Consolidated Station No. 3 in Hosston. The station was located on the west side of U.S. Highway 71 where it passes through the village. The man is unidentified. (Courtesy of the Jack D. Norman estate.)

In 1925, the Hart's Ferry Bridge was flooded where it crosses James Bayou, a Caddo Lake feeder bayou. In this view taken from the east side of the bayou, the bridge can be seen in the background center in front of two wooden oil derricks. The men in the boat are pulling it across the water by a rope that has been strung for that purpose. (Courtesy of the Jack D. Norman estate.)

The Gulf Refining Company of Louisiana developed wells on Caddo Lake 600 feet apart on 10-acre sites. Pilings were driven into the lake bed, drilling platforms and derricks were constructed, and drilling rigs were barged to the sites. In May 1911, the world's first over-the-water oil well, Ferry Lake No. 1, was completed. This c. 1920 photograph shows the well and others on the lake. (Courtesy of the Jack D. Norman estate.)

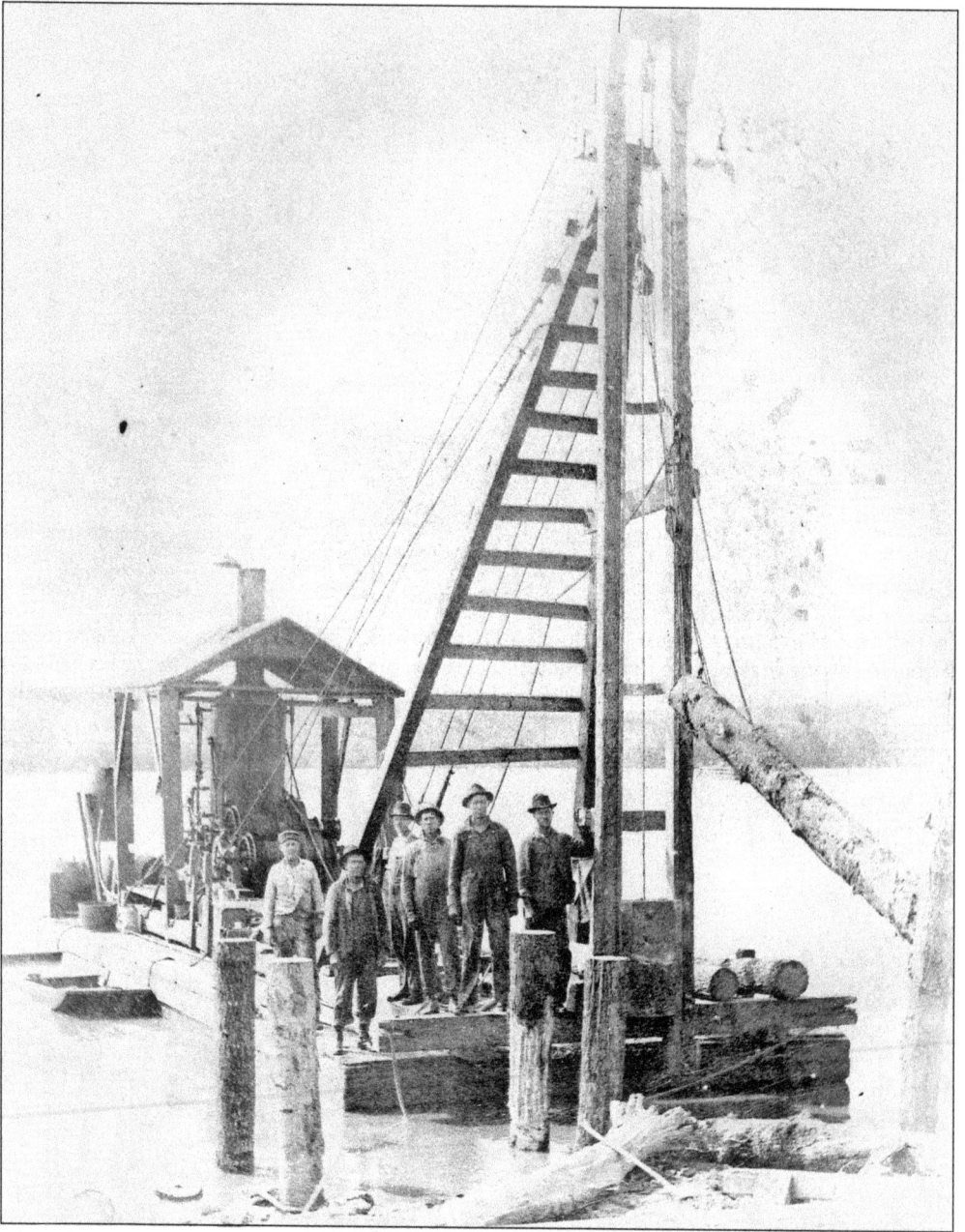

The pile driver was maneuvered to a well site on Caddo Lake. Then it drove large cypress timbers through the muck at the bottom of the lake and into the more solid earth underneath to create a sturdy framework upon which drilling platforms and derricks were constructed. Note that the mechanical force to move the weight was provided by a steam engine whose boiler is visible at the back of the skiff. (Courtesy of the Louisiana Oil and Gas Museum.)

Numerous successful oil wells were drilled and put into production on the lake, as this 1919 photograph shows. Some estimates put the total number of wells drilled on the lake at more than 200. It was in about that year that the amount of oil pumped reached a peak, and thereafter production began a steady decline. (Courtesy of the Jack D. Norman estate.)

This Caddo Parish Levee Board Treating Plant is pictured near Ida about 1920. Note the boiler and the storage tank in the rear center. The men are unidentified. (Courtesy of James Allison.)

Nature's wonders and man's industrial expression were uniquely combined in this 1920 reflective view of a wooden derrick on Caddo Lake. The lily pads in the foreground indicate the water's depth is no more than about 5 feet. There is a stand of bald cypress on the right and some deciduous trees on the left where the catwalk terminates. A small boat is tethered where the access ladder to the stand enters the water. (Courtesy of the Louisiana Oil and Gas Museum.)

More than 20 wooden oil well derricks in the Clear Lake area of the Caddo Field are seen in this 1925 photograph. As with Caddo Lake, the derrick was ubiquitous in north Caddo Parish. In the steamboat days, Clear Lake, located about where Oil City is today, was one of the bodies of water that constituted the route of travel for steamboats around the Red River logjam. (Courtesy of the Jack D. Norman estate.)

The Hart's Ferry Bridge across James Bayou was frequently flooded. The photograph is undated but was probably taken in the 1920s, and the lady standing in the right foreground was unidentified. The bridge runs left to right in the background, and the water is almost topping it. The bridge is along Louisiana Highway 2. (Courtesy of the Jack D. Norman estate.)

Many small, independent oil-refining companies were formed by the 1920s. One of those was the Union Refining Company that was located between Vivian and Trees. (Courtesy of the Jack D. Norman estate.)

The morning routine in 1914 for oil field roughnecks living at Trees included standing in line to get washed up before breakfast. Nightshirts, underwear, and all manner of dress were visible in the lineups. Along the left side of the photograph is a row of the dormitory-style tent houses the men lived in. (Courtesy of the Louisiana Oil and Gas Museum.)

Part of the Bayou State Refining Company in Hosston is seen in this 1958 photograph. Bayou State, headquartered in Shreveport, constructed the refinery in 1928 and was Hosston's only industrial business. By the 1980s, operations could no longer be economically sustained, and the equipment was dismantled and removed from the site. The site will soon be returned to its pre–oil boom woodlands beauty. (Courtesy of Melvin Giles.)

This 1950s view is of an Arkansas Louisiana Gas Company wellhead in the Rodessa field or, as it was colloquially referred to, a "Christmas tree." The gas went from the wellheads, into piping, and along the route compressor stations so that it could be moved to markets both in and out of state. (Courtesy of Mary Skaggs.)

These unidentified men are running surface casing on a well in 1936 during the second year of the Rodessa oil boom. Casing is a liner for the oil well that keeps it open by preventing cave-ins of falling earth and rocks along its depth. (Courtesy of the Jack D. Norman estate.)

Three

VILLAGES

A post office built adjacent to the railroad in 1896 ushered in the community of Rodessa. A depot was built there in 1936 at the start of the oil boom, and by 1940, the population exceeded 8,000 people. In 1967, Rodessa was incorporated, and today it has returned to the small village it was prior to the oil boom.

In 1897, J. R. Chandler sold a right-of-way to the railroad company and opened a post office in his store, naming it Ida after one of his daughters. A depot was built there in 1905. The Rodessa oil boom brought workers to the area, and by 1940, there were schools, churches, stores, and a movie theater. Ida was incorporated in 1967, and today its population is about 250.

James Hoss sold a railroad right-of-way through his property in 1898. In 1901, a post office was opened, and in 1902, a surveyor referred to the property as "Hosston." In 1905, a depot was constructed there. Soon mercantile stores, hotels, cotton gins, and a school were constructed. The oil fields brought workers and entrepreneurs to Hosston as well as its only industry: the Bayou State Oil Corporation. Hosston was incorporated in 1968.

No longer able to buy rights-of-way, the railroad company bartered with landowners to build depots and flag stations, naming them after the landowner. In 1898, Bob Gilliam agreed to the offer. A post office was located there in 1900, and in 1908, a tornado razed the village, killing 34 people. It was rebuilt and continues as a farming community. Gilliam was incorporated in the late 1960s, and today a cotton gin constitutes the local economy.

A few commercial enterprises began to cluster near a site along the railway in 1899. Land clearing brought planters and sharecroppers in. When a post office was opened in one of the homes in 1900, it was named Belcher after James Belcher, who was the majority landowner where the railroad had been constructed. In 1902, a depot was built in Belcher. The town was incorporated in the late 1960s and remains a small farming community.

In 1928, Malvin Williamson (left) and Pleasant Nichols were best buddies. They roamed about the small farming village of Rodessa finding fun wherever it could be had. Here they are shown in the yard of one of the sawmills that was located there. (Courtesy of Kathy Welch.)

Men came from far and wide to work as roughnecks in the Rodessa oil field. Here a young Centenary College of Shreveport student and athlete, Conway Baker, is working in 1935 on the Rodessa field's discovery oil well, Young No. 1. (Courtesy of Mary Skaggs.)

Standing together in 1941 are the men who brought in the last oil field boom of the area in 1935. On the left is R. W. Norton, the discoverer of the Rodessa field, the next two men are unidentified, and on the far right is I. L. Young, a store owner, on whose property the discovery well was completed. (Courtesy of Mary Skaggs.)

The second successful oil well drilled in the Rodessa field in 1935 drew a large crowd of spectators. The event that caused the gathering, other than the novelty of an oil well in those days, is unknown, and no one in the crowd is identified by name. They appear to be standing on a berm enclosing a slush pit. (Courtesy of the Jack D. Norman estate.)

45

This 1935 photograph is of Humble Company's Sanders No. 4 in the Rodessa field. Driller M Devini named the location Raccoon Camp. It is not known if the four men were roughnecks or if one of them was the driller. Note that by the 1930s, the oil well derricks were being made of steel rather than the wood timbers used during the previous two decades. (Courtesy of the Jack D. Norman estate.)

This 1936 view in the Rodessa field shows how the forests were cleared of all trees perhaps as far as 100 yards all around the well site. The tool pusher's shed is shown in the rear center behind the automobile. The pulley and hook suspended above the drilling platform indicates that either drilling or servicing was under way at the site. (Courtesy of the Jack D. Norman estate.)

A 1997 picture shows the 1939 Caddo Parish School Board–built Rodessa High School building. The high school was closed in 1955 when a new high school campus was built in Vivian that consolidated all of the high schools in north Caddo Parish. The structure languishes there today, waiting to be torn down. (Courtesy of Mary Skaggs.)

In the 1930s, Rodessa was a lively village that was growing, and stores were active all along the main street. Two steel derricks and the village's original water tower are shown behind the row of businesses. (Courtesy of the Jack D. Norman estate.)

Northwest Louisiana is in the area in the United States referred to as tornado alley. In 1937, one roared out of the clouds, striking Rodessa and causing widespread damage and injury. One survivor, then a very young boy, claims to have been carried about 100 yards in the air by the winds during the fury. Depicted is the destruction at an oil field supply business in Rodessa. (Courtesy of the Jack D. Norman estate.)

This location is probably at the present intersection of Louisiana Highways 1 and 168 in Rodessa. In the center foreground of the photograph, Nolan's Cash Store and the Broadway Hotel (left of the store) appear to be doing a booming business given the large number of vehicles parked in front of each one. (Courtesy of the Jack D. Norman estate.)

In 1936, the Vivian Oil and Gas Company extended it operations seven miles north to the village of Rodessa and opened a Sinclair gasoline service station. The two men on the right are probably operators of the service station given the hats they are wearing; none of the men are identified. Note that the station's lot was unpaved. (Courtesy of the Louisiana Oil and Gas Museum.)

Albert Alsup, in addition to being the engineer for the Black Bayou Lumber Company's train, was also a subsistence farmer and perhaps sold extra vegetables he grew to the commissary at the sawmill. He is shown on the left in this 1920 photograph on his farm north of the sawmill, next to him are his sons Guy (left) and Buddy; the man on the far right is unidentified. (Courtesy of David Welch.)

The man on the right, "Grandpa" Adam Stewart, was one of the first people to live in the village of Rodessa. The lady on the left is unidentified but is probably his wife. An Alsup family member donated the photograph, so he was probably an ancestor of Albert Alsup. (Courtesy Lillian Horton estate, Vivian Branch Shreve Memorial Library; photograph provided by Gladys Alsup.)

David Jonathan Evans and his wife, Lou Duskoa Evans, moved from Atlanta, Georgia, to north Caddo Parish near the future village of Ida in about 1866. The house is one of the earliest ones ever built in the area. It was later remodeled and was still in use in 1955. Depicted walking in the front of her home is "Aunt Duck" Evans. (Courtesy of James Allison.)

The Owens family, shown in this 1919 image taken in Ida, is, from the left to right, Wilburn, Ida, Lee (in her mother's arms), Allen, and Myrtle. When her father, J. R. Chandler, opened a post office in his store in 1897, he named the village Ida, after his daughter. The village that grew up around the post office came to be known as Ida as well. (Courtesy of James Allison.)

The 1902–1903 Bethsaida School photograph was taken at the school just outside of Ida. Surnames of the students included Daniels, Bain, Chandler, Herring, Slay, Allison, Hardin, Eubanks, Carrol, Austin, Prince, Summer, Whittington, Shaw, Preston, York, Burr, Moody, Stanley, and Brockman. School principal ? Barber is at the left rear. (Courtesy of James Allison.)

Ida's high school, built in 1905, was a magnificent wooden structure used for 25 years, at which point it was torn down and replaced by a brick school building. That school, like the one in Rodessa, was closed when the school district consolidated high school classes in 1955 in Vivian. (Courtesy of James Allison.)

The Bethsaida building functioned both as a schoolhouse and as the Bethsaida Baptist Church, whose congregation was captured on film in 1910. None of the congregants were identified in the photograph. It was very common for a church building to also be used as a school. (Courtesy of James Allison.)

William Wynn homesteaded a section of land in north Caddo Parish in about 1870. Later he, with others, was responsible for building a school and a church for the growing number of settlers beginning to move nearby. Depicted in the photograph are Wynn's daughters, Mamie (left) and Mina (right). Mamie later married a gentleman surnamed Bain, and Mina's husband was from the Iles family. (Courtesy of James Allison.)

D. H. Evans and his wife are shown in this c. 1920 photograph. They were among the many early settlers of Ida. (Courtesy of James Allison.)

The 1912 photograph shows some of the Bethsaida Baptist Church's congregation. Surnames of the members included Whittington, Haldeman, Chandler, Keel, Evans, Whittington, Trant, Hortman Lester, Perdue, Byrum, Bumgardner, Bain, Murphy, Hanson, Slay, Bryant, Gryder, and Sams. (Courtesy of James Allison.)

In 1909, the Standard Oil Company built a pump station in Ida along its pipeline to boost the oil from the fields in Oklahoma on toward its refinery in Baton Rouge. After 1935, another pipeline was added that connected to the Rodessa oil field. The engine and pump house was photographed in 1999. (Courtesy of James Allison.)

The Westmoreland family built their home in Ida in 1908 in the classic Victorian style of the era. From left to right are Maggie Westmoreland, Barney Westmoreland, Mary Chandler, Ada Westmoreland, Burney Westmoreland, Silas Ratliff, and Harrison Westmoreland (sitting on the steps). (Courtesy of James Allison.)

In 1917, the sawmill at Kiblah, Arkansas, appears to have a full yard of stacked lumber ready to go to market. Kiblah was located at the state line in Arkansas, and Ida is located at the state line in Louisiana. The sawmill is located in the background of the picture. (Courtesy of James Allison.)

Ida experienced a spurt of growth because of the 1935 Rodessa oil boom. A few businesses, a hotel, and other similar enterprises were added for the oil field workers. The amount of activity seen in this street scene is more than the village experiences today. (Courtesy of James Allison.)

The Hoss family poses in 1904 in front of their home. Seated on the ground, from left to right, are Connie, Sam, unidentified, Tim, Madie Worley, and Martha Hoss. Standing at the far right is Emma Hoss, the mother of James Hoss Jr. James sits on the horse behind the group. The village was named for Emma's husband, James Hoss Sr. The man sitting on the horse in the left background is unidentified. (Courtesy Hosston Branch, Shreve Memorial Library.)

An 1885 photograph shows James Hoss Jr. with his sister Consuello, who later married into the Worley family. (Courtesy Hosston Branch, Shreve Memorial Library.)

The first public school in Hosston was built in 1900 on property donated by the Hoss family; the building still stands today. By 1919, a six-room school had been constructed on an adjacent site for grades 1 through 10. In 1931, a new, brick school was constructed. (Courtesy Hosston Branch, Shreve Memorial Library.)

In the left foreground of this 1912 picture of Hosston is the Barn Hotel; to the left of it is the Hosston Mercantile. Beyond the railroad tracks to the right of center is the Woodman Hall. To the left of that is the Allen Mercantile. In the far right background is the Community Church and to the far left are the Field Saw Mill and mill houses. (Courtesy of Melvin Giles.)

Shown in 1910 are some of the businesses located in Hosston. In the left center is the railroad depot, and to its right, the two-story building is the Allen Mercantile. To its left is a barbershop. No other structures are identified. Note the two horsemen in the extreme left center, and behind them, adjacent to the depot, is the village's water well. (Courtesy of Melvin Giles.)

58

Joe Lloyd is sitting on his wagon in front of the icehouse, which was adjacent to the Hosston Mercantile Company. Ice was delivered by train from Shreveport, where it was then stored in facilities like these in area communities. In 1990, Lloyd's widow, Myrtle Lloyd, then 91 years old, assisted in providing identifying information for many of the people and structures in this series on Hosston. (Courtesy of Melvin Giles.)

Samuel Hoss Jr. lived from 1887 until 1917. He may have been a casualty of the First World War. (Courtesy Hosston Branch, Shreve Memorial Library.)

This c. 1920 photograph was taken in front of a Hosston business. The couple on the left is unidentified; the lady on the right is Emma Hoss. (Courtesy Hosston Branch, Shreve Memorial Library.)

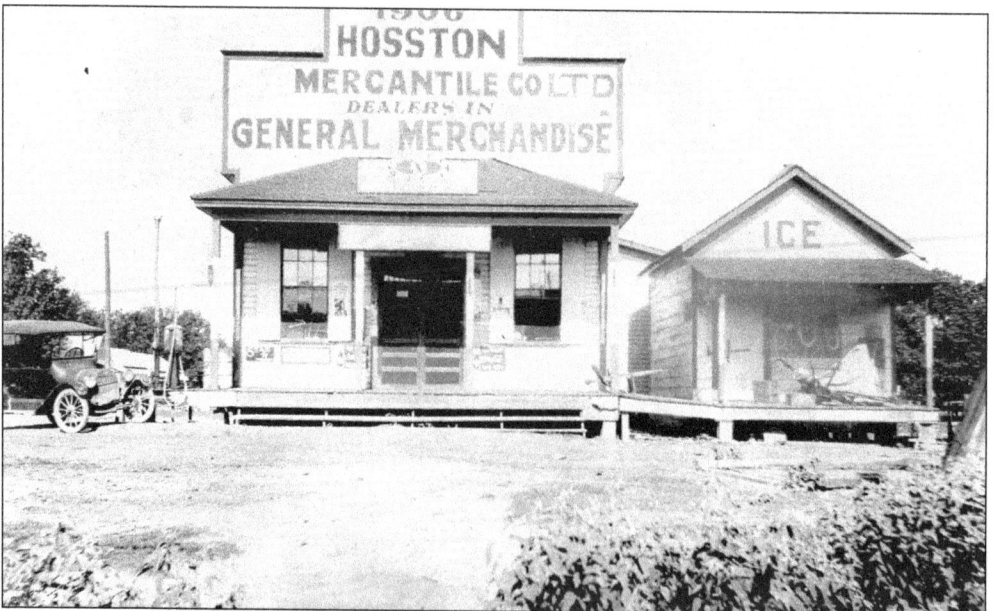

The Hosston Mercantile Company, founded in 1906, was a major enterprise in the early days of Hosston. Note the early model vehicle and gasoline pump at the left front corner of the store. (Courtesy of Melvin Giles.)

This trio of hunters appears to have had a successful hunt during the winter of 1920 in the Hosston area. From the left are Olin Roberts, Hardy Lummus, and Lawton Roberts. (Courtesy of the Jack D. Norman Estate.)

Martha Hoss, daughter of Sam and Viola Hoss, is shown standing in front of the family's automobile. The Studebaker is displaying a Louisiana license plate, dated 1925. (Courtesy Hosston Branch, Shreve Memorial Library.)

Among the public transportation assets available to the citizens of Hosston was the 1920s-era Shreveport Auto Livery. Joe Lloyd is looking out a passenger window, and driver Joe Federucci is at the steering wheel. This livery is No. 18, and to contact the company, one needed to only dial their telephone number, 73. (Courtesy of Melvin Giles.)

Until a few decades ago, high school seniors would stage a play just prior to graduation. It was an event enjoyed by the teachers, the community, and especially the seniors. The 1947 Hosston High School senior-class actors are, from the left to right, Lou Whately, Robert Spain, Jimmy Wilson, Johnny Pistole, J. C. Boydston, Dorothy Adcock, Garner Herring, Gene Owens, June Camp, Lorene Long, and Nancy Dominick. (Courtesy of Johnny Pistole.)

The daughter of Sam and Viola Hoss, Martha, is shown in her 1917 baby picture. (Courtesy Hosston Branch, Shreve Memorial Library.)

Martha Hoss graduated from Hosston High School in 1934. (Courtesy Hosston Branch, Shreve Memorial Library.)

The Wilhites were another prominent family in Hosston during the first few decades after the village's founding. From left to right are (seated) Everett and Minnie Lee; (standing) Caroline, Henry, Sudie, Louis, and Modine. (Courtesy of Johnny Pistole.)

Three young men from Hosston posed on a photographers set at the 1947 annual Louisiana State Fair, still held in Shreveport. The three banditos, from left to right, are J. C. Boydston, Gene Owens, and Johnny Pistole. (Courtesy of Johnny Pistole.)

Two members of the prominent Hoss family and their wives are shown in this 1925 photograph. Sitting in the front are Sam and Viola Hoss, and standing at the rear are Minnie and Tim Hoss. (Courtesy Hosston Branch, Shreve Memorial Library.)

The Worley and Hoss families were related by marriage. This 1890s photograph depicts Sam Hoss Sr. sitting in front of unidentified members of the Worley family. (Courtesy Hosston Branch, Shreve Memorial Library.)

The Hosston High School 1946–1947 school year band is shown on stage in the high school auditorium. The band members are unidentified. Standing at the left rear is the school principal Preston Allison (left) and band director James Lee. (Courtesy of Johnny Pistole.)

Standing in the front are Martha Hoss (left) and Sam Hoss. The unidentified children standing at the rear are members of the Worley family. (Courtesy Hosston Branch, Shreve Memorial Library.)

This view captures some of the impact the Caddo oil boom had on Hosston. Four oil well derricks rise over the community. The one on the right stands behind the first brick building that was built in the village. (Courtesy Melvin Giles.)

Standing in front of the Hosston Garage are the owners Doc and Gladys Hemperly. The man walking at the far left is Joe Lloyd. The garage sold Goodyear tires and Texaco gasoline to its customers and was one of the first garages in the village. (Courtesy Melvin Giles.)

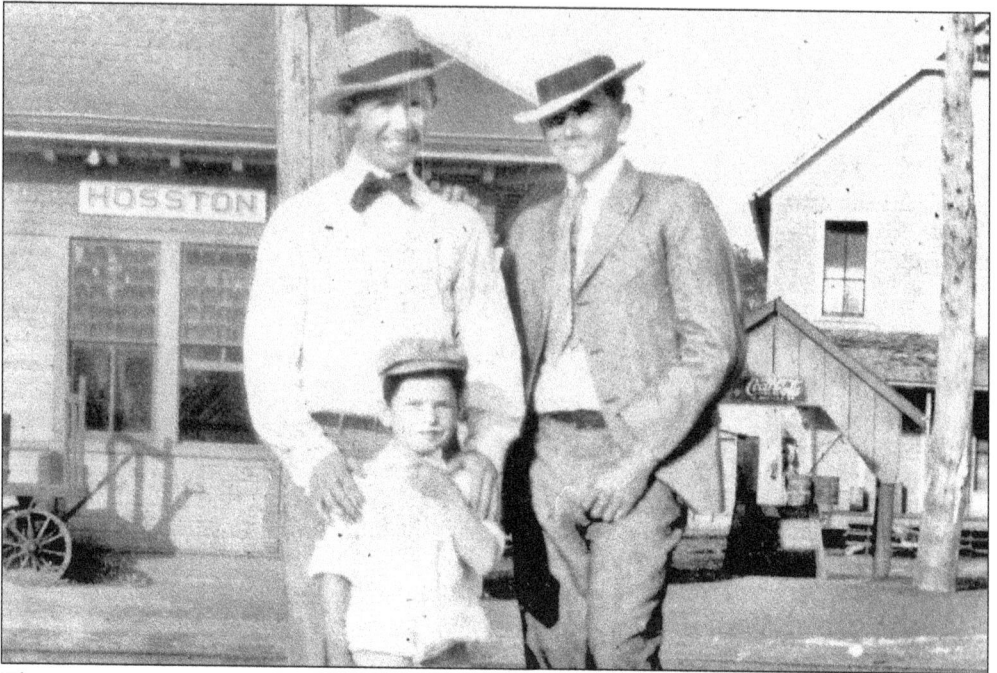

This young boy's name is Erastus, and he is standing in front of his uncle Jidd Fuller. Standing at the right is Robb Stansberry. They are in downtown Hosston, standing at the rear of the railroad depot in this *c.* 1925 picture. A baggage cart is partially visible at the depot. (Courtesy Melvin Giles.)

The crowd is gathered around Hosston's Shreveport Auto Livery stop at the rear of the railroad depot. From left to right are the (Diamond) Jim Peak store, Jim Hoss' store, the Barn Hotel (background right center), and Hosston Mercantile. Just discernible is a water well, whose curbing is visible, at the left front of the Hoss store. (Courtesy Melvin Giles.)

Four

TOWNS

Separated in time by about 60 years, three towns—Mooringsport, Vivian, and Oil City—in north Caddo Parish evolved because of different economic movers. Ultimately they all grew from their village roots into towns because of the same force: the petroleum industry.

In 1842, Timothy Mooring began a for-fee ferryboat service across Caddo Lake. By 1845, steamboats left Shreveport, went up Soto and Caddo Lakes and Cypress Bayou to Jefferson, Texas, and stopped at Mooring's Port along the way. Mooringsport became the first community in north Caddo Parish to become permanently settled. Famous folk song writer and singer Hudie "Leadbelly" Ledbetter of mixed Native American and African American blood was born here in 1888 and is buried in the Shiloh Cemetery just south of the town. Mooringsport was incorporated in 1927.

In 1896, the Kansas City Southern Railway bought land to build a town adjacent to their right-of-way and filed the plat as the town site of Vivian. The railroad company built a depot and marketed lots in the town site. This town site boom brought many businesses and people to Vivian, and it grew rapidly. Between 1900 and 1910, the village's population doubled because of the 1906 oil boom, and in 1910, it was incorporated as a village. In 1911, ninety-two new homes were constructed. In 1912, Vivian was incorporated as a town, and by 1914, three major oil companies had located offices there. Vivian's population doubled again between 1930 and 1940 because of the Rodessa oil boom.

The community that sprang into being in 1906 around the first oil well in the area grew very rapidly. In 1907, a post office was opened in the community's only store, and it was named Oil City after the evolving petroleum industry. All the social ills of an oil boomtown were soon present and mixed with the workers, their families, and petroleum-specific trades and shops. Oil City even temporarily had its own red-light district. In 1940, as the boom faded, Oil City was incorporated as a village, and in 1958, it became a town.

In 1922, a destructive and dangerous fire erupted along and in some structures on the east side of Oil City's railroad tracks. This view looks south from the railroad tracks. Spectators are huddled beyond the smoke on the left, and the depot is depicted in the right center. (Courtesy Louisiana Oil and Gas Museum.)

The Oil City Restaurant and Rhodes' Pharmacy were located along Land Avenue in Oil City in this 1912 photograph. People are going about their activities with the many businesses shown. (Courtesy Louisiana Oil and Gas Museum.)

From left to right are Bell the dog, Gordon, Myrta, and Mrs. Hal Boylston. The tent-top-and-wood-frame-side structure is typical of family housing during the first 10–20 years of the Caddo oil boom. (Courtesy Louisiana Oil and Gas Museum.)

Families lived and homesteaded where they could find available land. In 1910, this family lived on the shores of Caddo Lake. Here is an unidentified family with their livestock and fowl. There appears to be a smokestack on the houseboat behind them. Perhaps they lived on the houseboat. (Courtesy Louisiana Oil and Gas Museum.)

The Oil City Drug Company's unidentified owners are shown inside their store during the 1930s. Notice the molded-tin ceiling and walls that are highly prized today. (Courtesy Louisiana Oil and Gas Museum.)

An unidentified couple, dressed to the nines, must have been on Caddo Lake for a Sunday afternoon boating experience. Behind the lady, a typical over-the-water oil-production site with various buildings, storage tanks, and the wooden derrick is shown. (Courtesy Louisiana Oil and Gas Museum.)

Another scene of Oil City depicts the vibrancy of a growing community in 1912. Beyond the horse-drawn wagons on the left is the Dixie Mercantile Company, and beside it is the Phoenix Hotel. The Kansas City Southern Railroad depot is on the right. (Courtesy Louisiana Oil and Gas Museum.)

During the 1922 Oil City fire, business owners and families moved what household and other effects they could onto the railroad tracks for preservation. The photograph was taken from atop a railroad car with a northward view. (Courtesy Louisiana Oil and Gas Museum.)

The railroad referred to the flag station at the first structure in Oil City as "Ananias," and locals referred to it as "Surrey," since a horse-drawn surrey frequently met wealthy oil company men there. The sign on the front of the building read, "Post Office and Murray's Store." In the foreground from left to right are Carrie Player, an unidentified boy, and Robert Player. The others are unidentified. (Courtesy Louisiana Oil and Gas Museum.)

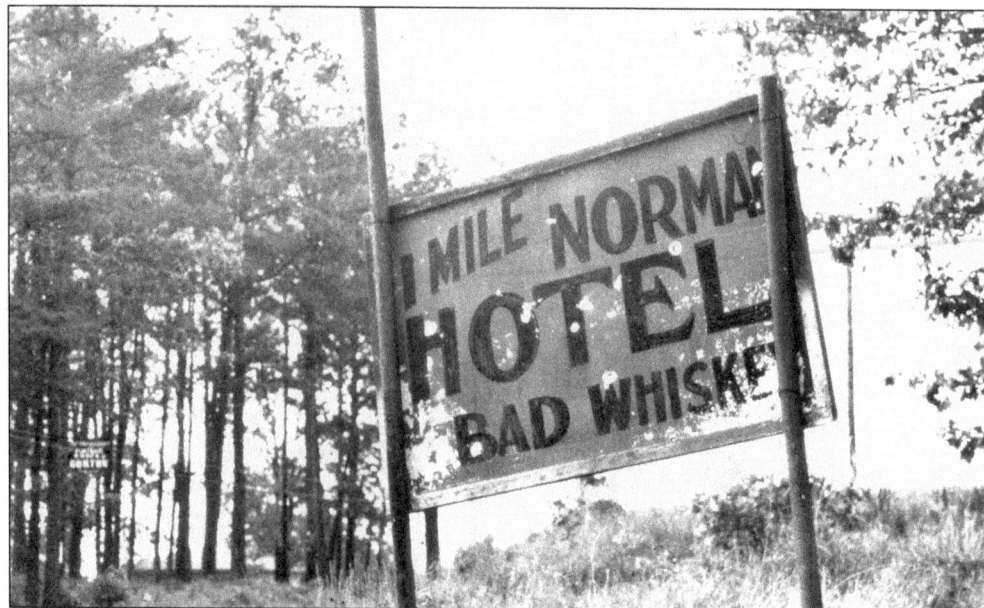

The Norman Hotel was one of a few hotels in Oil City. This amusing sign was located adjacent to the highway south of town and advertised their bad whiskey. Note the numerous bullet holes in the sign. (Courtesy Louisiana Oil and Gas Museum.)

Pitts Landing was located east of Oil City on the shore of Caddo Lake. This 1910 or 1911 photograph shows the buildings there and some unidentified ladies. Earlier in time, steamboats had occasionally conducted business at the location. (Courtesy Louisiana Oil and Gas Museum.)

Before the streets of Oil City were paved, they frequently became nothing more than muddy roads, as shown in about 1922. More of the downtown area is shown, and on the right are Bob's Smoke House and a store owned by J. Maritzky. Wingo's Pharmacy was located inside the store, and just down the street, RCA Victrolas could be purchased. (Courtesy Louisiana Oil and Gas Museum.)

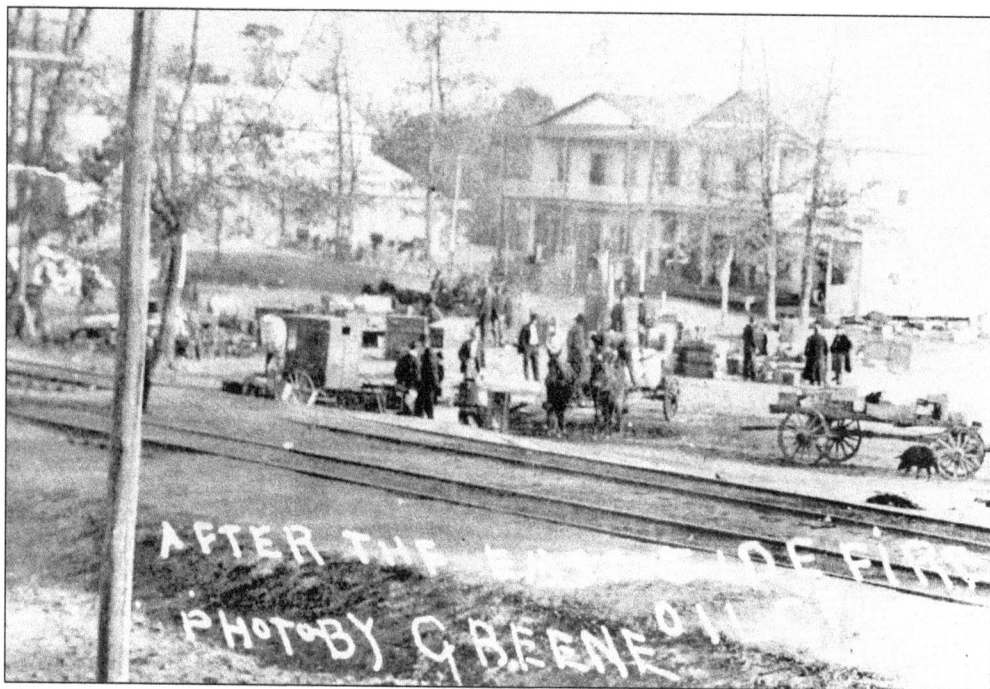

The aftermath of the 1922 east Oil City fire shows that building contents still remained adjacent to the tracks. Undoubtedly the people were planning on how to rebuild and to salvage what property they had saved. Note the hog rooting about underneath the wagon at the right center of the photograph. (Courtesy of the Jack D. Norman estate.)

A well-stocked, unnamed department store in Oil City seems to have offered most frequently used goods. Note, at the back, there was also a grocery department. Obviously multiple product lines being sold in a single location was not a new concept. (Courtesy Louisiana Oil and Gas Museum.)

An unidentified family and their dog are enjoying a day of fishing on Caddo Lake in the 1930s. Note the oil well derricks in the background. Caddo Lake is still a popular and productive fishery. (Courtesy Louisiana Oil and Gas Museum.)

A confirmation class of the St. John Catholic Church in Oil City posed in 1920 on the steps of the church. The identification of class members and others has been lost. (Courtesy Louisiana Oil and Gas Museum.)

Both male and female sports teams competed at Oil City High School. Shown is the 1935 girls' basketball team. None of the girls can be identified. (Courtesy Louisiana Oil and Gas Museum.)

The George family was one of the earliest to settle in the area that was to become Oil City. In 1918, Effie Jones George proudly displays her impressive stringer of what locals refer to as "bream" or "brim," which are various types of small sunfish. (Courtesy Louisiana Oil and Gas Museum.)

From 1824 to 1841, the Caddo Indian Agency paid for the operation of a ferry at Mooringsport. In 1842, Timothy Mooring began his for-fee service nearby. Both operated near where these unidentified men are ferrying oil field equipment across the lake about 1910. The railroad trestle at the left is the second one built there, and the automobile bridge has yet to be built. (Courtesy Mooringsport Mini Museum.)

In 1909, two fishermen, Tom Allen and Will Teel, discovered pearl-bearing mussels in Caddo Lake around the slopes of Cypress brakes and near the lake's northern shoreline. People swarmed to the lake to find mussel pearls. One pearl sold for $1,500. Most pearlers were not as lucky, and by 1914, when the lake was dammed near Mooringsport, the pearl craze was over. These unidentified men are trying their luck at pearl hunting. (Courtesy Mooringsport Mini Museum.)

Fritz Heinisch (left) and Bud McWilliams are riding on the *Grey Goose*, their pleasure boat, on Caddo Lake about 1915. (Courtesy Mooringsport Mini Museum.)

Sachiniko Cha Murata, one of the most successful pearl hunters on Caddo Lake, owned this party boat, referred to without malice as "Jap's boat." The swimmers were all members of a local Boy Scout troop enjoying a day on the lake in 1928. (Courtesy Mooringsport Mini Museum.)

Mooringsport's east side is depicted here in 1915. The gentleman walking along the tracks on the left is unidentified; behind him is the water tank that supplied the railroads' steam engines. Behind that is the Mooringsport depot. This perspective looks north, showing the primarily residential area of the village. The second white house from the right in the center belonged to the Croom family. (Courtesy Mooringsport Mini Museum.)

This 1914 photograph dubbed Mooringsport "The City of Derricks." This perspective looks south along the tracks. On the left is the depot, and on the right is the business district. On the right is the Terry-Jordan Lumber Company, and left of it is the C. A. Parrot Staple and Fancy Grocery Store. (Courtesy Mooringsport Mini Museum.)

In August 1913, the Star Oil Company's Loucke No. 3 near Mooringsport came in as a gusher. Not long afterwards it caught fire shooting a monstrous column of smoke and flames high into the air. At a loss of 30,000 barrels each day, it was the single largest oil well fire in the history of the country. (Courtesy Mooringsport Mini Museum.)

The Gulf Oil Company's blacksmith's shop is depicted in Mooringsport in about 1918. Charles Wilgus, wearing the leather apron, is standing at the far right in the photograph. (Courtesy Mooringsport Mini Museum.)

Throughout the Caddo oil field, the equipment used in production was moved by various animal locomotive means. In 1915, an unidentified worker is moving an oil barrel using a four-mule team near Mooringsport. (Courtesy Mooringsport Mini Museum.)

The Mooringsport Bank, a branch of the Continental Bank and Trust Company, is shown in 1925. The bottom line of the sign painted on the bank's left front window proclaims "Strangers Welcome." The bank was robbed in 1921 and closed in 1929. The Gulf Oil field office occupied the second floor. (Courtesy Mooringsport Mini Museum.)

Huddie Ledbetter, of mixed Native American and African American blood and popularly known as "Leadbelly," was born on the Jeter Plantation in 1888 at Mooringsport. He was an important folk-song writer and singer, having penned, among others, "Goodnight Irene," "Rock Island Line," and "Midnight Special." Leadbelly died in 1949 and is buried in the Shiloh Cemetery south of Mooringsport. (Courtesy Mooringsport Mini Museum.)

In the spring of 1934, heavy rains resulted in Caddo Lake's flooding. This view in Mooringsport shows how high the water rose in that year, as it was almost completely covering the Gulf Oil Company warehouses. Typically the water is 20 to 25 feet below the traffic lane of bridge in the background. (Courtesy Mooringsport Mini Museum.)

This remarkable photograph captured a highly attended baptism ceremony conducted by the Mooringsport Baptist Church at the foot of the traffic bridge in Mooringsport in 1915. Automobiles and pedestrians are strung along the traffic bridge, and other observers lined up along the shoreline and out over the water in boats. Within the arc defined by the boats and the people onshore, the preacher can just be seen performing the baptismal rite. (Courtesy Mooringsport Mini Museum.)

A tornado struck the Mooringsport area on June 10, 1941. The Mooringsport Methodist Church, built in 1868, sustained moderate to heavy damage as a result. Part of the tiling of the church's roof was torn off, and what appears to be part of the steeple or bell tower is lying in front of the church. (Courtesy Mooringsport Mini Museum.)

This beautiful structure, shown in about 1920, was located on the shore of Caddo Lake, just west of Mooringsport proper. A ballroom and dining room were located on the first floor, and bedrooms were upstairs. On Saturday nights, dances were held there, and at various times civic and church functions were hosted. (Courtesy Mooringsport Mini Museum.)

James Noel was an early settler, businessman, and head of a prominent Mooringsport area family. Noel and his brother Richard bought many hundreds of acres of land south of Mooringsport and owned and operated a general store and a cotton gin in the village. The steamboat landing at the village was at Noel's Point. Noel was a Confederate veteran of the Civil War and is buried in the Mooringsport Cemetery. (Courtesy Mooringsport Mini Museum.)

D. B. Binford's Bargain Store in Mooringsport offered "ice cold lemonade, soda pop, and cider," as seen in this 1900 photograph. Clearly the picture was taken during the holiday season, as the banner proclaims "Santa-Claus in Full Blast." Just under the roof's peak, the sign, Noel Bros, shows that Richard and James Noel had owned the 1869-built building. (Courtesy Mooringsport Mini Museum.)

The original First Baptist Church of Mooringsport was built by Aley Flanagan and his son Kit in 1920. It had a large auditorium, a choir loft, six Sunday-school rooms, and a baptistery. (Courtesy Mooringsport Mini Museum.)

Timothy Mooring is the namesake of the town of Mooringsport. He is shown here in a c. 1860 photograph. Mooring was born in North Carolina in 1801, moved to Tennessee in the late 1820s, and subsequently moved to Louisiana in 1837 to become the first settler in north Caddo Parish. The 1839 state survey shows a Mooring's clearing a few miles south of Caddo Lake. In 1842, he began to operate a ferry across Caddo Lake, and his south-shore location at Noel's Point soon became Mooring's Port, a steamboat port. His wife's mother was born a Croom, and two of Timothy's daughters married into the prominent Noel and Croom families. Mooring died in 1880 in Webster Parish, Louisiana. (Courtesy Mooringsport Mini Museum.)

The first school in Mooringsport was a one-room structure built in 1885 wherein all grades were taught. None of the teachers or students in this photograph are identified. (Courtesy Mooringsport Mini Museum.)

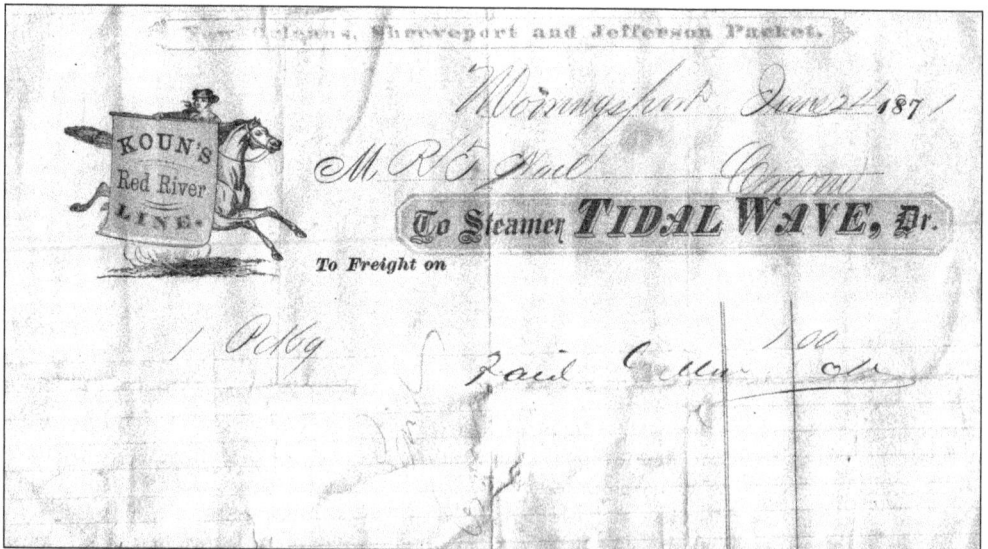

Noel and Croom surnames both appear on a receipt issued at Mooringsport in June 1871 for freight shipment charges on the steamer *Tidal Wave*. The boat belonged to the Koun's Red River Line. The men paid $1 for the shipment of one package. (Courtesy Mooringsport Mini Museum.)

Fishermen are seen boating under the vertical lift draw section of the Mooringsport traffic bridge that was built in 1914 and spans Caddo Lake. It was a one-lane traffic bridge that served the community for almost 80 years until it was replaced by a safer, two-lane span. The bridge remains in place and was put on the National Register of Historic Places in 1996. (Courtesy Jack D. Norman estate.)

Mooringsport's new brick school was built in 1911 and remains there today. The original 1885 school building was torn down, and this one was constructed in the same location. (Courtesy Mooringsport Mini Museum.)

This view of oil wells on Caddo Lake was captured in the 1930s from the bluff at Mooringsport looking north. Note the catwalk that extends from the well site at the right center of the photograph all the way across the lake to the shoreline on the left. (Courtesy Mooringsport Mini Museum.)

A Kansas City Southern steam engine–pulled train is crossing Caddo Lake in this c. 1912 picture. The traffic bridge was yet to be built. What appears to be a pedestrian walkway across the shallow lake spans the picture in the foreground. (Courtesy Mooringsport Mini Museum.)

This 1913 Greene and Grueter photograph depicts what they referred to as a "bird's-eye view of the Derrick City, Mooringsport." Wooden derricks are strewn throughout the village proper, interspersed among the houses and businesses. (Courtesy Mooringsport Mini Museum.)

A passenger train is shown stopped at Mooringsport's depot in about 1910. An unusually large crowd is shown near the facility. Perhaps many were spectators of the recent, novel means of transportation in the area. The G. B. Croom store is shown in the left background. (Courtesy Mooringsport Mini Museum.)

This is another view showing how prevalent the oil well derricks were throughout Mooringsport. The children sitting in a row on the fence are unidentified. (Courtesy Jack D. Norman estate.)

The Oil and Fuel Company's wells are shown on the lake in 1914. Mooringsport is located in the forest of derricks and trees in the background. What function was performed in the building with the three steam or smoke stacks is not certain. (Courtesy Mooringsport Mini Museum.)

The Atlas Oil Company's landing below the train bridge at Mooringsport was flooded by high water in the spring of 1914. Oil well casing pipes are shown both left and right of the stack of logs. Behind the log stack is Atlas's pile driver, used to construct the stable support structure for drilling platforms. (Courtesy Jack D. Norman estate.)

This 1916 view looking to the northwest is of the newly constructed vertical lift drawbridge at Mooringsport. The derricks in the background, beyond where the two points of land narrow the body of water, are on what is referred to as the "big lake" part of Caddo Lake. (Courtesy Jack D. Norman estate.)

The first bridge for railroad traffic across Caddo Lake built in 1895 at Mooringsport was so low that spring floods covered it at times. A boardwalk was built between the crossties for pedestrian use. During floods, a man slowly felt his way walking across the trestle preceding the train to make sure the crossing was safe. The higher and safer bridge replaced this one in 1910. (Courtesy Jack D. Norman estate.)

A. H. Teat is shown in 1912 in front of his short-order restaurant on Louisiana Avenue in the town of Vivian. (Courtesy Lillian Horton estate, Vivian Branch Shreve Memorial Library; photograph provided by Ouida Castello.)

Maude Heath (left) and Scott Satterwhite, children of prominent residents and business owners in Vivian, are shown in a c. 1912 portrait. (Courtesy Lillian Horton estate, Vivian Branch Shreve Memorial Library; photograph provided by Scott Satterwhite.)

The Liverman Grocery was another early business in Vivian. Depicted from left to right are Mrs. Liverman, Mrs. Dave Barr, ? Barr, and Carrol Liverman, owner. (Courtesy Lillian Horton estate, Vivian Branch Shreve Memorial Library; photograph provided by Merle Liverman.)

Before 1900, A. M. Solley operated a sawmill about three miles west of Vivian. Solley was one of the earliest settlers in Vivian, and by 1900, he owned and operated a general mercantile business in the town. (Courtesy Lillian Horton estate, Vivian Branch Shreve Memorial Library; photograph provided by Juanita McDuff.)

Between 1935 and 1938, Vivian mayor J. D. Bickam got a bond issue for $13,000 to fund street paving. That was initiated in 1937, and it covered six blocks of the downtown area. The paving of Front Street is shown. Note the Ritz Theater in the far right background of the picture. (Courtesy Lillian Horton estate, Vivian Branch Shreve Memorial Library; photograph provided by Iva McMillan.)

The office of the Southwestern Gas and Electric Company, predecessor of the Arkansas Louisiana Gas Company, was located on West Front Street in Vivian. Standing in the front are Marie Parker (left) and Clyde Parker; behind them are Fred Parker and an unidentified child (sitting on the post); standing in the doorway is Mrs. Parker, who was company superintendent. (Courtesy Lillian Horton estate, Vivian Branch Shreve Memorial Library; photograph provided by Mrs. Fred Parker.)

Henry Thomas was of the earliest automobile owners in the town of Vivian. Here he is seen sporting around in his 1914 Ford Cabriolet on Louisiana Avenue. (Courtesy Lillian Horton estate, Vivian Branch Shreve Memorial Library; photograph provided by Henry Thomas.)

J. K. Heath built Vivian's first electric plant in his backyard in 1910. The company's generator came every day at 5 a.m., and its loud exhaust awoke everyone nearby, negating their needs to have alarm clocks. For a while, Heath's daughters, Jewell and Lillian, operated the candy and ice cream shop (at left). (Courtesy Lillian Horton estate, Vivian Branch Shreve Memorial Library; photograph provided by Jewell Heath.)

Switzers Yellow Jacket Company sold candies, orangells, cocotels, and silk ice cream in their Vivian shop. Standing from left to right are R. L. Gilbert, unidentified, Mrs. Will Hardin, Garland Hardin, Lillie Hardin, Willie Hardin, and unidentified. (Courtesy Lillian Horton estate, Vivian Branch Shreve Memorial Library; photograph provided by Mrs. J. W. Bentley.)

Shown is a 1914 view of Louisiana Avenue looking east from Pine Street. The two-story brick building on the right was the Vivian State Bank. On the left side of the street were the Bank of Vivian, two hotels, and the Spell building (listed from left to right). In the background center is the depot, having just undergone an expansion. (Courtesy Lillian Horton estate, Vivian Branch Shreve Memorial Library.)

The original depot was built in Vivian in 1895 and is shown before 1900. In about 1910, it was enlarged, as shown in the preceding photograph. Note that behind the depot, only a single house had been constructed in the downtown area at this time. (Courtesy Lillian Horton estate, Vivian Branch Shreve Memorial Library.)

In February 1912, Eckhart the balloonist and aerial daredevil brought his show to Vivian. The balloon, surrounded by an expectant crowd, is seen on Front Street as it is being filled with gas. The railroad depot is seen to the right of the balloon. (Courtesy Lillian Horton estate, Vivian Branch Shreve Memorial Library; photograph provided by J. C. Harrell.)

William Browning established his plantation just west of Vivian using slave labor to construct the house in 1848. The Browning house is the only one in the area that predates the Civil War. The picture shows a 1911 Browning family reunion in front of the house. Browning descendants still live in the house today. (Courtesy Lillian Horton estate, Vivian Branch Shreve Memorial Library; photograph provided by Lloyd Browning.)

The Little and Stephens store was located at the corner of Front Street and Louisiana Avenue in Vivian. The owners wear white shirts and appear in the doorway in this 1908 picture; Little is holding the duster, and Stephens is leaning on the doorway. The others are unidentified. The store sold dry goods, men's clothing, and repaired watches. (Courtesy Lillian Horton estate, Vivian Branch Shreve Memorial Library; photograph provided by E. R. Burr.)

This is a better view of Vivian's depot in 1914, after it was expanded to accommodate the growing town. Two large rooms for cargo and baggage were added to the north side of the original structure. The view is from the north. (Courtesy Lillian Horton estate, Vivian Branch Shreve Memorial Library.)

In about 1905, a water well for nearby business and family use was completed in the center of Louisiana Avenue, just west of Vivian's railroad depot. It was curbed and featured a roof. Note the unevenness of the dirt street and the weeds scattered down the street. (Courtesy Lillian Horton estate, Vivian Branch Shreve Memorial Library.)

The Thomason Lumber Company store was located on Louisiana Avenue in Vivian where the town's square is now situated. Standing from left to right are an unidentified salesman, W. J. Thomason, his wife, two unidentified women, Raymond Thomason, and Doss Bickham. (Courtesy Lillian Horton estate, Vivian Branch Shreve Memorial Library; photograph provided by Boyd Thomason.)

106

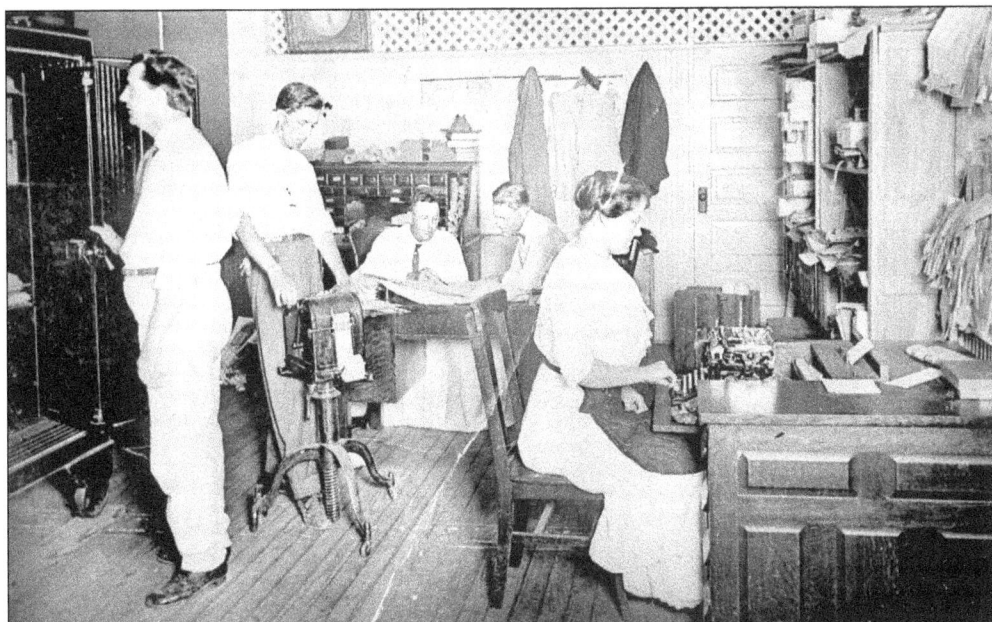

The office and business area of Thomason's lumber company shows employees operating business machines of the times. W. J. Thomason, wearing a tie, is seated at his desk. The other office personnel are unidentified. The man to left of Thomason is operating a portable, height-adjustable adding machine. (Courtesy Lillian Horton estate, Vivian Branch Shreve Memorial Library; photograph provided by Boyd Thomason.)

Eight members of Vivian's bicycling club are shown here about 1901 on Louisiana Avenue. From left to right are Watts McLemore, Raymond Thomason, Tom Williams, Willie Williams, Jack Porterfield, Jim Jeter, Nay McLemore, and Oscar Dell. The McLemore bicyclers were the children of James G. McLemore, physician, pharmacist, and Vivian's first mayor. Doctor McLemore's office is at the right in the photograph. (Courtesy Lillian Horton estate, Vivian Branch Shreve Memorial Library; photograph provided by Boyd Thomason.)

Woodmen of the World chapters were known as camps. Two Shreveport camps, the Broad Axe and Maple, celebrated at Vivian's picnic grounds in 1912. The camps' banners are shown at the back of the crowd. The man under the "x" drawn on the picture was R. B. Baker, Vivian's mayor between 1912 and 1914. No others were identified. (Courtesy Lillian Horton estate, Vivian Branch Shreve Memorial Library; photograph provided by Boyd Thomason.)

W. J. Thomason was a major economic influence in Vivian. Shown is his commissary. (Courtesy Lillian Horton estate, Vivian Branch Shreve Memorial Library; photograph provided by Bernice Barr.)

Shown at their Vivian home is the W. J. Thomason family. Thomason is clearly the mustachioed gentleman sitting in the back; unfortunately none of the others were identified. Note the goat-drawn wagon that was popular amusement for children. (Courtesy Lillian Horton estate, Vivian Branch Shreve Memorial Library; photograph provided by Bernice Barr.)

W. J. Thomason's sawmill was located just off of Arkansas Avenue in Vivian. Thomason is in the right foreground of the picture. (Courtesy Lillian Horton estate, Vivian Branch Shreve Memorial Library; photograph provided by Bernice Barr.)

R. C. Carroll, having been duly elected, was sworn in as the village of Vivian's first marshal in April 1910. That is also probably the year that Vivian was incorporated as a village. (Courtesy Lillian Horton estate, Vivian Branch Shreve Memorial Library; photograph provided by Dixie Johnson.)

The Standard Oil Company's service station was located at Georgia Avenue and Pine Street in Vivian. In this 1928 photograph, standing from left to right are Fred Alsup and Horace Kendrick, the station operator. The Model T roadster in the background was owned by Alsup, and the pickup belonged to Howard Adger. (Courtesy Lillian Horton estate, Vivian Branch Shreve Memorial Library; photograph provided by Alicia Wilson.)

The children living southwest of Vivian were bussed to school in a Ford Model T school bus. W. M. Leach, the driver, is shown with his bus. (Courtesy Lillian Horton estate, Vivian Branch Shreve Memorial Library; photograph provided by A. B. Hanner.)

A gentleman named Pyron is shown standing in the yard of his home on Louisiana Avenue in 1912. (Courtesy Lillian Horton estate, Vivian Branch Shreve Memorial Library; photograph provided by Dixie Johnson.)

The Dixie Drug Company was one of the three that operated in Vivian. Inside the store in the 1920s are, from left to right, B. H. Williams, H. W. Garrett, C. H. McEachern, N. B. Terry, and J. D. Gerald. (Courtesy Lillian Horton estate, Vivian Branch Shreve Memorial Library; photograph provided by H. W. Garrett.)

The Christian family lived in the home on the left, and the other one belonged to Walt Taylor. The homes were located on the west side of Pine Street, two blocks from downtown Vivian. Note the model airplane in flight at the center forefront of the picture. (Courtesy Lillian Horton estate, Vivian Branch Shreve Memorial Library; photograph provided by Clyde Lee.)

This photograph of Billy (left) and Ted Butler was taken before 1920. Behind them is the First Baptist Church of Vivian, constructed in 1905. W. J. Thomason's lumber barn is in the right background. (Courtesy Lillian Horton estate, Vivian Branch Shreve Memorial Library; photograph provided by Clyde Lee.)

Phillip Kottle used his given name to identify his five-and-dime store in Vivian. Inside Phillip's five-and-dime, from left to right, are Mrs. Brown Oxford, Mrs. Marvin Kennedy, two unidentified women, and Phillip Kottle. (Courtesy Lillian Horton estate, Vivian Branch Shreve Memorial Library; photograph provided by Phillip Kottle.)

The members of the First Baptist Church had their new brick facility constructed in 1921. The home of Tycus Hart was located at the rear of the church. (Courtesy Lillian Horton estate, Vivian Branch Shreve Memorial Library; photograph provided by Henry Thomas.)

The Dixie Drug Company's store is shown under construction in the 1920s. The sign on the adjacent building reads, "Drink Atlas Special Brew." Atlas was a Chicago-based brewery during Prohibition that produced beer with 3.2 percent alcohol. (Courtesy Lillian Horton estate, Vivian Branch Shreve Memorial Library; photograph provided by Henry Thomas.)

In about 1920, Benjamin Minshew leased the Solley building on Front Street; he refurbished it and opened it as the movie theater. A lady is looking out of the telephone office window on the second floor. The signage on the Cherokee Strip Model T bus, an advertising gimmick for the theater, indicates that a special movie was to be shown that day. (Courtesy Lillian Horton estate, Vivian Branch Shreve Memorial Library; photograph provided by Henry Thomas.)

This view of 1930s Vivian was captured from atop the original water tower in the town. Louisiana Avenue is on the right and runs eastward to its terminus at the town's depot. (Courtesy Lillian Horton estate, Vivian Branch Shreve Memorial Library; photograph provided by Henry Thomas.)

The Pelican Tool Supply Company engineered and manufactured tools and materials for the area's petroleum industry. The building still stands today on the east side of the railroad tracks downtown. (Courtesy Lillian Horton estate, Vivian Branch Shreve Memorial Library; photograph provided by J. H. Bentley.)

T. F. Cochran, his wife, and their daughter were photographed in 1915 in the yard of their home on Louisiana Avenue in Vivian. (Courtesy Lillian Horton estate, Vivian Branch Shreve Memorial Library; photograph provided by J. F. Cochran.)

The disastrous 1911 oil well fire at Harrell No. 7, about six miles southwest of Vivian, became a spectator attraction. A group of Vivianites have boarded a wagon for a trip to the fire. The man wearing the black hat under the ink-penned X on the wagon was Dan Crowe. His daughter Kathryn was to his right. (Courtesy Lillian Horton estate, Vivian Branch Shreve Memorial Library; photograph provided by Dan Crowe.)

Eckhart suspended himself upside down tethered to a balloon. The balloon is almost ready to be launched from near the depot in Vivian in 1912. The man astride the horse was Claude Harrell, and his son, J. C., sat behind him. Standing in front of the horse from left to right were Jeff Hartzo, Grover Paine, and Lee Cauley. (Courtesy Lillian Horton estate, Vivian Branch Shreve Memorial Library; photograph provided by J. C. Harrell.)

The home of Jasper Land was located on East Louisiana Avenue in Vivian. Notice the tents used for housing behind the Land home. This was during the second decade of the 20th century. (Courtesy Lillian Horton estate, Vivian Branch Shreve Memorial Library; photograph provided by J. H. Bentley.)

J. C. Harrell stands on the fence at the left, and his sister Luna stands on the fence at the right of the gate. Standing in the gate opening is Grover Paine, a half brother of the children's father, Claude Harrell. Harrell used the barn to stable team horses, which he rented to move oil field equipment in the area. (Courtesy Lillian Horton estate, Vivian Branch Shreve Memorial Library; photograph provided by J. C. Harrell.)

118

An African American minstrel performance is under way on Louisiana Avenue in 1920s photograph of Vivian. Across the street from left to right are a bank, two hotels, a grocery, and the T. S. Spell building. (Courtesy Lillian Horton estate, Vivian Branch Shreve Memorial Library.)

The third bank in town was the Bank of Vivian, located at Louisiana Avenue and Pine Street. The Dixie Studio and K. A. Sinclair Cash Store operated out of the right side of the structure. (Courtesy Lillian Horton estate, Vivian Branch Shreve Memorial Library.)

The first bank located in town was the 1907 Vivian State Bank on Front Street. The men in the photograph are unidentified. The owners of the bank were brothers G. M. Huckaby, president, and H. H. Huckaby, vice president. Will Caldwell was their cashier. (Courtesy Lillian Horton estate, Vivian Branch Shreve Memorial Library.)

The interior of McKeever's blacksmith shop in Vivian is shown in this 1914 photograph. From left to right are McKeever, unidentified, Herman Hammock, and unidentified. (Courtesy Lillian Horton estate, Vivian Branch Shreve Memorial Library.)

Tax dollars were hard at work in this view of Frank James asleep under his Model T dump truck. James was employed by the Louisiana State Highway Department. (Courtesy Lillian Horton estate, Vivian Branch Shreve Memorial Library; photograph provided by Henry Thomas.)

The clerks at the Little Palace sundries shop were Toppye Malone (left) and Myrtis Reed. (Courtesy Lillian Horton estate, Vivian Branch Shreve Memorial Library.)

The electricity generating plant building built by John Heath in 1910 for downtown businesses was incorporated as Vivian Light and Power in 1914 and was sold to Gulf Public Utilities in 1925. Heath's 1914 structure stood for many years and was demolished about 50 years ago. (Courtesy Lillian Horton estate, Vivian Branch Shreve Memorial Library.)

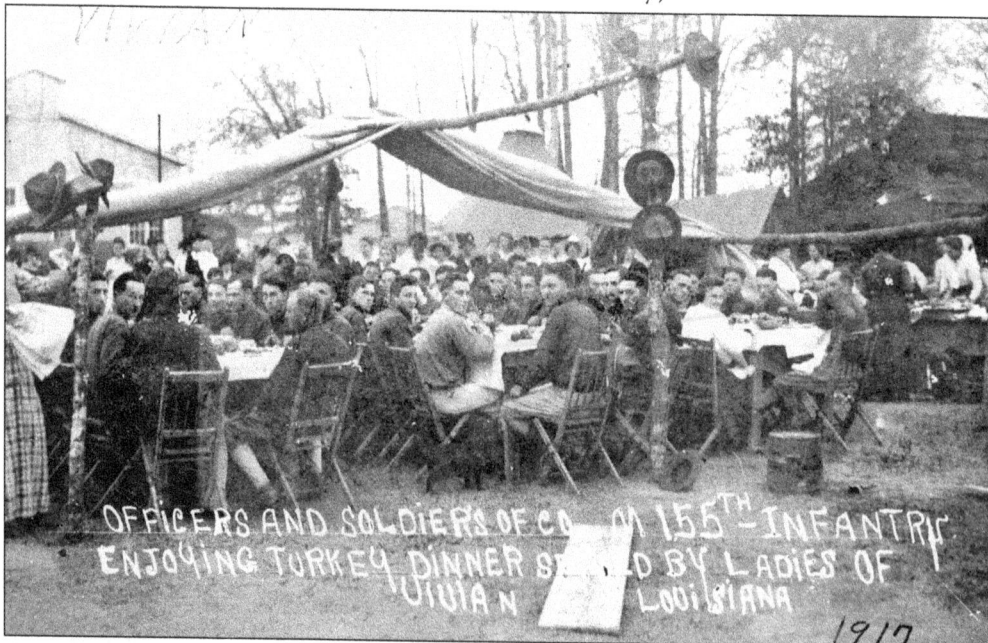

Oil field workers unionized in 1917 and went on strike at the Trees oil field. To preclude repeating earlier violence in the field, Company M of the 155th Infantry was sent to keep the peace. Their local camp was in downtown Vivian. To show their support and appreciation, the ladies of Vivian prepared and served the troops their 1917 Thanksgiving dinner. (Courtesy Lillian Horton estate, Vivian Branch Shreve Memorial Library.)

This is the Tycus Hart home on Pine Street as it appeared in 1920. Hart operated a ferry across James Bayou, and the location is still referred to as Hart's ferry. In 1906, he sold his plantation near James Bayou to William Stiles, who later developed the village of Trees at the site. (Courtesy Lillian Horton estate, Vivian Branch Shreve Memorial Library.)

This view of A. M. Solley was at his Vivian home on Arkansas Street about 1915. Today the area behind him is a residential neighborhood. Where his sawmill was located west of town is known as Solley's hill. About 1922, he terminated Benjamin Minshew's lease on his building on Front Street and operated it for a short while as a movie theater. (Courtesy Lillian Horton estate, Vivian Branch Shreve Memorial Library; photograph provided by J. C. Harrell.)

T. F. Holt's livery, feed, and stable business was located on Front Street across from the railroad station complex. He is the man holding the two horses in the picture; the others are unidentified. (Courtesy Lillian Horton estate, Vivian Branch Shreve Memorial Library; photograph provided by Frances Holt LaCaze.)

This is Vivian as it looked about 1910 from Arkansas Avenue east of the railroad looking northwest. The roof of the depot is just visible behind the warehouse structure in the foreground, and behind it is Holt's Livery. Beyond that, the steeple of the First Baptist Church is visible, and to the right of it is the Tycus Hart home in front of the Vivian School. (Courtesy Louisiana Oil and Gas Museum.)

124

A typical school bus is shown as it was used during the first three decades of the 20th century. The people depicted are unidentified. (Courtesy Jack D. Norman estate.)

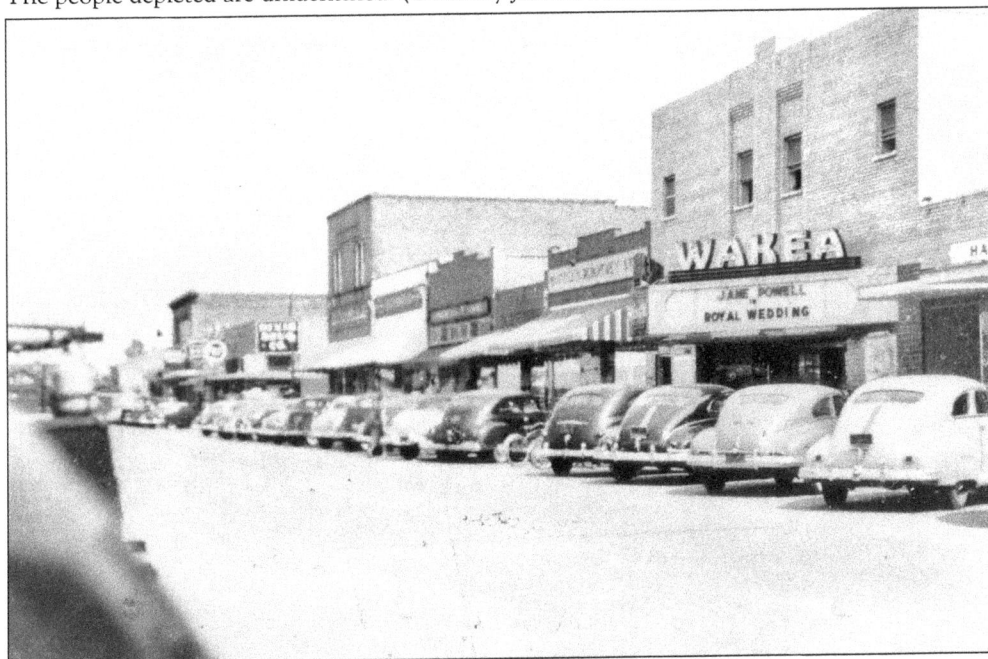

A busy downtown Vivian is depicted in this 1950s scene, in which businesses and cars lined both sides of Louisiana Avenue. After A. M. Solley terminated Benjamin Minshew's 1920 lease, Minshew constructed and opened the Fox Theater on Louisiana Avenue in 1925. After his death, his son continued to operate it as the Rialto. In 1945, he sold the theater, and it continued to operate as the Wakea. (Courtesy Louisiana Oil and Gas Museum.)

Cotton was and continues to be an important crop in north Caddo Parish. A typical cotton field is shown here about 1910, where both black and white pickers have just filled a wagon that awaits transport to the gin. (Courtesy Jack D. Norman estate.)

The T. S. Spell building is on the left in this 1915 image, and two freight rail cars are seen parked on a side rail at the depot where unloading took place. The streets of Vivian would not be paved for another 20 years. (Courtesy Jack D. Norman estate.)

The Moonshine Pharmacy also sold cold drinks, as its sign states in front of the Front Street location about 1915. The signs on the windshields of the Model Ts state, "The Hustler." The cars were probably used in a local taxi service of that name to transport men to and from work sites in the area and for in-town services. (Courtesy Louisiana Oil and Gas Museum.)

Street maintenance is performed on Louisiana Avenue in 1918. J. R. Hardin's Grocery store is on the left next to W. O. Williams's business. The two-story building is the Vivian State Bank, constructed in 1913. (Courtesy Louisiana Oil and Gas Museum.)

Visit us at
arcadiapublishing.com

....